My Pakistani family history

Vic Parker

Heinemann
LIBRARY

young
Explorer

www.heinemann.co.uk/library
Visit our website to find out more information about Heinemann Library books.

To order:
- ☎ Phone 44 (0) 1865 888066
- 🖹 Send a fax to 44 (0) 1865 314091
- 💻 Visit the Heinemann Bookshop at www.heinemann.co.uk/library to browse our catalogue and order online.

First published in Great Britain by Heinemann Library, Halley Court, Jordan Hill, Oxford OX2 8EJ, part of Harcourt Education. Heinemann is a registered trademark of Harcourt Education Ltd.

Editorial: Charlotte Guillain
Design: Joanna Hinton-Malivoire
Picture research: Erica Martin
Production: Duncan Gilbert
Illustrated by Jacqueline McQuade
Originated by Modern Age
Printed and bound in China by South China Printing Co. Ltd.

ISBN 978 0 4310 1508 8 (hardback)
ISBN 978 0 4310 1503 3 (paperback)

12 11 10 09 08
10 9 8 7 6 5 4 3 2 1

British Library Cataloguing in Publication Data
Parker, Vic
My Pakistani family history. - (Family histories)
305.9'06912
A full catalogue record for this book is available from the British Library.

Acknowledgements
The publishers would like to thank the following for permission to reproduce photographs:
© Alamy pp. **18** (foodfolio), **22** (Photofusion Picture Library), **23** (Craig Holmes); © Margaret Bourke-White p. **9** (Time & Life Pictures/Getty Images); © Ashley Cooper p. **14** (Alamy); © Corbis p. **20** (Ashley Cooper); Getty Images pp. **7**, **26 top** (Time & Life Pictures/Margaret Bourke-White), **17**, **19** (Hulton Archive), **24**, **26 bottom** (Photonica); © Popperfoto.com pp. **12**, **13**

Cover photograph of Bhartis family reproduced with permission of © Superstock (Bananastock).

Every effort has been made to contact copyright holders of any material reproduced in this book. Any omissions will be rectified in subsequent printings if notice is given to the publishers.

Contents

Words appearing in the text in bold, **like this**, are explained in the Glossary.

Imran's family history

My name is Imran. I am nine years old. I live with my mother, father, brother, and sister in a city called Manchester.

Manchester is in the north of England.

Pakistan is in South Asia, near India, China, Afghanistan, and Iran.

My family comes from a country called Pakistan. Pakistan is large, with mountains, plains, forests, and deserts. Some areas can have floods while other areas have **droughts**. It can be very hot in the summer and freezing cold in the winter.

My family tree

My mother's parents

Muhammad Ali
(my grandfather)
born 1944

Fatima Bibi
(my grandmother)
born 1946

My father's parents

Mustafa Sharif
(my grandfather)
born 1939

Parveen Bibi
(my grandmother)
born 1943

My grandparents grew up in Pakistan. One of my grandfathers, Muhammad Ali, lived in an area called the Western Punjab. The Punjab region of Pakistan has five rivers running through it. The water makes the land excellent for growing crops.

Village boys were
often taught outdoors.

My grandfather Muhammad lived in
a village of cotton farmers. He and the
other boys spent only a little time at
school every day. They were needed
to work in the cotton fields.

My grandfather lived with his parents, two brothers, and three sisters.

My grandfather's home was built around a courtyard with a well in the middle. The kitchen was in one corner, but sometimes food was cooked outside. There were stairs going up to the roof, where people sometimes slept. The toilet was also on the roof.

In Islam, boys and men often pray separately from girls and women.

My grandfather and his family were **Muslim**. They followed the religion of Islam. They said prayers five times every day. Each Friday they went to pray in a holy building called a mosque.

While my grandfather and his brothers worked in the cotton fields, the girls in the family had jobs to do around the home. They had to clean and cook, fetch water and firewood, and feed the chickens and goats.

The family sold their cotton for money to buy food.

My family tree

Muhammad Ali
(my grandfather)
born 1944

Fatima Bibi
(my grandmother)
born 1946

My great-grandparents chose a bride for my grandfather when he was young. She was a village girl called Fatima. They got married when my grandfather was 18 years old. Fatima came to live with my grandfather and his parents in their house.

During my grandfather's childhood, there was a lot of fighting between Pakistan and the neighbouring country of India. People fought over which bits of land belonged to which country. Many people were forced to leave their homes.

Millions of people in Pakistan and India became **refugees**.

My grandfather and great-uncle arrived in Britain with just a few clothes and possessions.

Many people from Pakistan went to Britain for a better life. They could earn much more money in Britain. Many Pakistani men had been in the British army and were used to travelling. My grandfather and my great-uncle decided to go to Britain too.

This cotton mill is like the one where my grandfather worked. It is closed down today.

In 1964, my grandfather and great-uncle arrived in a town called Burnley, to work in a **cotton mill**. They rented a small house with several other men from Pakistan. It was difficult to fit in with the local people because my grandfather and great-uncle spoke Punjabi, not English.

My family tree

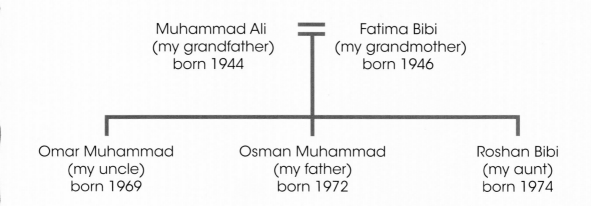

Muhammad Ali
(my grandfather)
born 1944

Fatima Bibi
(my grandmother)
born 1946

Omar Muhammad
(my uncle)
born 1969

Osman Muhammad
(my father)
born 1972

Roshan Bibi
(my aunt)
born 1974

My grandfather and great-uncle saved up hard for three years. Then they sent money for their wives to travel to join them. Soon, both couples had children. My grandfather and grandmother had two boys and a girl.

My grandfather and great-uncle set up a shop together. It sold all sorts of things from food to cleaning products to paper and pencils. The two families lived together in a flat over the shop.

My father grew up with his cousins, as well as his brothers and sisters.

My grandfather grew up in a large Pakistani **community**.

My father was brought up speaking Punjabi at home but at school all his lessons were in English. Some of his friends were from Pakistani families and others were from British families.

One of my father's favourite foods was **samosas**.

My grandmother and great-aunt always cooked Pakistani food. My father enjoyed *saag* dishes, which are made from spinach, and *daal*, which is made from lentils.

My grandparents wore clothes called *shalwar kameez*, which is a long shirt over loose trousers. My grandmother and great-aunt also covered their heads with scarves. But my father did not want to wear traditional Pakistani clothes. When he was a teenager, he liked British fashions.

In the 1970s it was fashionable for men to wear wide collars and very flared trousers.

By the time my father left school, my grandfather and great-uncle had opened three supermarkets. My father was manager of one of these shops. But he also went to college at night to study business.

The supermarkets sold both Pakistani and English food.

A Pakistani wedding is called a *shadi*.

My father met my mother, Qulsum, through friends of the family. She worked as a **designer** in her family's clothes business. The families held a party when the couple got **engaged**. When they got married, the wedding celebrations lasted for three days.

Several other families from Pakistan live in our street.

My father got a job as a businessman in Manchester. He and my mother went to live there in their own house. It has a big living room, three bedrooms, and a small garden.

My parents wanted to have children straight away. First my brother and sister were born, and then me. My mother stopped working so she could look after us.

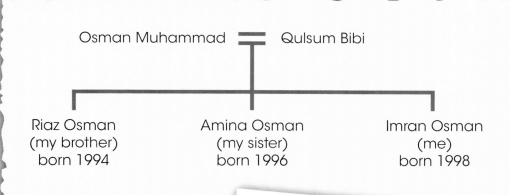

Osman Muhammad ═══ Qulsum Bibi

Riaz Osman	Amina Osman	Imran Osman
(my brother)	(my sister)	(me)
born 1994	born 1996	born 1998

I took this photograph of my brother and sister a few years ago.

23

At my school in Manchester there are lots of children whose families once came from Pakistan. I would like to visit Pakistan one day.

My favourite subject at school is PE. I want to play cricket when I grow up.

I speak English with my cousins, but I speak Punjabi with my grandparents.

I often see my cousins, aunts and uncles, and grandparents. We have big meals together in our homes or sometimes at restaurants. I like being part of a big family.

Then and now

My grandfather spent very litle time in school because he had to work in the cotton fields. I go to school every day and enjoy lots of different subjects.

My grandfather grew up in a house together with his aunts, uncles, cousins, and grandparents. I don't live with all my relatives but we get together very often.

Imran's family tree

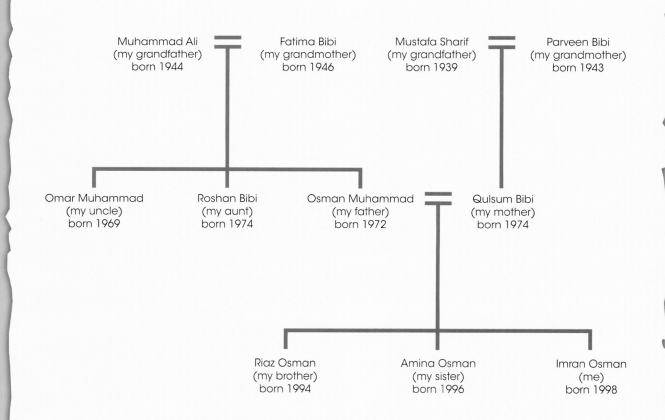

Muhammad Ali
(my grandfather)
born 1944

Fatima Bibi
(my grandmother)
born 1946

Mustafa Sharif
(my grandfather)
born 1939

Parveen Bibi
(my grandmother)
born 1943

Omar Muhammad
(my uncle)
born 1969

Roshan Bibi
(my aunt)
born 1974

Osman Muhammad
(my father)
born 1972

Qulsum Bibi
(my mother)
born 1974

Riaz Osman
(my brother)
born 1994

Amina Osman
(my sister)
born 1996

Imran Osman
(me)
born 1998

Finding out about your family history

- See if your family members have any photographs of when they got married, or when they were young. You could turn the photographs into a family history scrapbook. Get your family to write their memories next to the photographs.

- Ask your family about what life was like when they grew up. What toys did they like to play with? What food did they like to eat? What were their friends like? Did they go through difficult times? You could record them talking or write down what they tell you.

- Ask your mother, father, aunts, uncles, and grandparents to help you make your own family tree.

- Look at a map and draw circles around the places where your family has lived. Find out about those places through books and websites. See if your family can take you on trips there.

More books to read

P is for Pakistan, Shazia Razzak (Frances Lincoln, 2007)

We're from Pakistan, Emma Lynch (Heinemann Library, 2005)

Websites

www.bbc.co.uk/history/walk/memory_index.shtml
This website gives you tips on finding out about your own family history.

http://pbskids.org/wayback/family/tree/index.html
This website helps you to put together your own family tree.

Glossary

community group living in a particular area or sharing the same background

cotton mill factory where raw cotton from cotton plants is turned into cotton thread and cotton material

designer person whose job is to decide what style things should be made in, such as clothes, food packets, cars etc.

drought period of very dry weather when there is a severe shortage of water

engaged when a couple get engaged, they promise to get married

Muslim person who follows the religious teachings of the prophet Muhammad. They belong to the religion of Islam.

refugee person who has had to run away from their home, leaving everything behind, because they are in danger

samosa pastry snack filled with meat or vegetables

Index